BEST-SELLING J

CW00971410

WAYNE KOESTENBAUM

BEST-SELLING

JEWISH PORN FILMS

TURTLE POINT PRESS : NEW YORK : 2006

ISBN 1-885586-43-4   LCCN 2005926847

Design and composition by Jeff Clark
at Wilsted & Taylor Publishing Services

CONTENTS

I

II

III

V

VI

FOR STEVEN MARCHETTI

1

STANZAS IN MY 39TH YEAR

WHY I WANT X IN MY 39TH YEAR

I used to be pretentious;
then I grew simplistic.
Should I devote myself
to pleasure or to labor?

I dreamt of a deep thinker:
Rousseau? A moment ago
I had the idea (it escaped)
that almost saved my life.

I love concentrating,
hugging a periphery
or a hole:
I wish I could prove it.

Somebody strong circled
the word "was" when it occurred
three times in one sentence.
I might have been the figure circling "was."

APHORISTIC IN MY 39TH YEAR

I wonder if I have scandalous doings (an early botched
marriage) to reveal
tabloid-style in a poem
and thereby charm the world.

Doubt it.
I was miserable and then
wrote a strict
opus one in C.

RITARDANDO IN MY 39TH YEAR

Without license I drove
a bad car in the dark.
I kissed and saved the pieces
in an envelope and slowed down.

My mother telephoned the room
where my brother and I
slept and played Schumann.
Sick of delays

I said, "Unless the composer
intended them, I'm skipping
ritards in this piece,
we don't want it to drag on longer than it should."

ROLE MODEL IN MY 39TH YEAR

I nominated my role model for a Nobel Peace Prize
in Woodstock. Who could blame her
for offering me a bite of lemon meringue pie?
At the cramped diner she eased

herself into a long meditation on our distance
from the rock 'n' roll era;
my body temperature dropped below the cistern
level the role model decreed adequate for schizos.

She'd retired from the civilized world
to pursue theory. Her maiden name:
Valium. She massaged my buttocks
and promised warm compresses that never came.

Today, my black wool sweater smells
of stalagmites and pauses:
my role model wore it on an ocean liner—
waters damned by omissions, equally damned by gold . . .

PRINCESS DIANA IN MY 39TH YEAR

I walked a Hamptons beach.
Diana approached. I stopped,
backtracked, performed reconnaissance.
"Well, look who's here," she said.

We claimed a corner table at the beach club
and met my relatives—aunt drinking mirabelle,
uncle offended by Diana misusing a Yiddish phrase.
He plugged his book; the princess turned away.

She told me, "I'm grateful
for the affair. Over the years
I've given your evasions much thought."
What evasions, Diana?

MAYORAL RACE IN MY 39TH YEAR

I dropped out of the mayoral race:
a scandal. Offered
the democratic nomination,
I begged to be left alone,

I gave up every ruse.
Standing upright, I napped.
Everyone said, "He looks awake!"
But I was fast asleep.

NOTHING IN MY 39TH YEAR

My face is widening,
cheeks a clown's.

Lazy, slow, without ambition,
yesterday I met

a man with breasts
and beautiful

slick Johnny
Stompanato hair:

I swallowed his
incomprehensible propaganda.

I wish I had a larger chin:
it could function as stop sign.

THE POURQUOI CLUB

LANA

Wounded, prosaic, she trusted
gentle people, like me.

We used to think she was a joke—
now she's widely cited as an expert

on time. *Lana held open
her peignoir* . . . Is Crisco kosher?

I hid her raincoat in my closet for one year—
then she called to claim it, and we met

for coffee in a blizzard.
We discussed the HIV-positive stud

who advertises. I wonder if his clients worry.
Lana, I miss loquacity's Lourdes.

RAIN SCENE

"Cantilevered" describes
my pregnant mother's outward-tending leg.

Rosemary Clooney has some trait
in common with what's-her-name:

limited vocal endowment? Sorry
I'm so depressed: it's the mouse

droppings by the cardboard box.
I look forward to meeting the fatherly director

who might give me permission retroactively
to retake the rain scene in his famed bad movie

about a different east, a farther north
south, somewhat west of where we stand.

I can't find the Ned Rorem
sea songs in the card catalogue,

and the librarian won't let me enter the stacks.
Those three songs have a blue tinge.

Unfortunately, they don't exist—
I dreamt them.

He wrote hundreds of real songs.
Why can't I content myself with those?

A highfalutin violinist loved them, too,
and forgave me for freezing her out.

POSH

My father said a Latin mass, using his "posh" accent.
Then, at a hotel window, looking down

to Madison Avenue, he wept:
I was stuck with complete sentences.

After my father's window weeping spell
his face was young again, like Walter

Benjamin's. Walking the rose garden's
thorned periphery, he didn't smile.

Slowed down, thick with thought,
he wore green clip-ons, green jacket.

Much about him was green.
Occasionally a cheerful man pierced my abstraction.

There's no point in re-recording the tenor
repertoire: in 1942 it expired.

AUDREY

I called Audrey Hepburn from a subway pay phone.
She reported horrid marriages on the veldt.

No one understood what Audrey had been through!
Then I called Liz: "Audrey praised you to the skies."

I insinuated myself into Liz's favor
by dropping Audrey's name. Darkling

on the Gatsby patio during the snowstorm
Liz wandered in a white pop dress, ignored

hypersexed bride, her hymen a bother.
Who else did I become as I fell backward?

Knowing how to spell
got me far. But I can't spell indispensable.

ABORIGINES

My father was born in 1928
to native German parents

near Uncle Tom's Cabin,
seriously! My father's father

never discovered his proper vocation—
broken by war and expatriation,

he sold postcards of nude aborigines:
greetings from Caracas.

I told a student, curtly,
"Define empathy." I miss station

wagons, driving them while stoned past midnight.
Someone should invite me to a poetics

symposium in Florence or Taos;
I have much to say about spontaneity.

ARLES

In 1980 before Steve and I started sleeping
together I dreamt he drove me to Arles.

In the movie *Les Demoiselles de Rochefort*
starring Catherine Deneuve and her sister Françoise

Dorléac, either Deneuve or Dorléac sings the word
"pourquoi" stickily, so Steve and I sing

14

a sticky "pourquoi"
while we drive from Germantown

to Rhinecliff. We're charter
members of the pourquoi club.

Dorléac died in a car crash, June 26, 1967,
shortly after completing *Les Demoiselles*.

Three lost books I never wrote:
Hotels. Joseph Cornell and His Mother. Bathrooms.

Our summer grass is golden-gray and dry.
Steve whistles along with Petula Clark's *"Mon Homme."*

BULLETINS

BULLETIN FROM THE VACANT LOT

A sadist crawled through my apartment window
to steal four jelly glasses

and found, on my body, a small round area,
like a yo-yo, worth vibrating.

If my head and stomach weren't throbbing
I'd be a worthwhile stop on the "Homes of the Stars" bus tour.

I live near a Rite Aid.
Now I must go babysit the rain.

BULLETIN FROM THE BRONCHIAL PASSAGES

A blonde triathlon athlete,
victor of previous meets,

rammed her petite head
against a fence and cried

"Bring me a balanced meal!"
At her behest I chopped

parsley and olives
but hid the cornucopia:

I didn't want her
to know I was alive.

BULLETIN FROM THE BOTTOM OF THE SEA

"Structure," says the cat—
that's why I love cats.

Flowers on a hillside in May,
my virginity:

if I thought it would do any good . . .

A man fixes
my window with his window:

our windows
rub together.

Only the sights
hanging from my eye

occur to me.
To reach farther is

his window's
hubris, now mine.

BRIEF BULLETIN

Often she said "brief"
in the middle of sex, to infuse

it with honey,
cream of tartar?

Our attitudes toward school
fun differed. Emotionless,

I gave brief answers
and, like a hunk, stared down the horizon.

BREACHES AND IMPROPRIETIES

THE COLLECTED WORKS OF SLIMBOY

One cloacal day, a Princess
Margaret rose opens.

My mother smokes—
but never in the car.

Has she room in her
wide heart for my perfidy?

She can't fry a simple
sausage without trembling

but she has the power to step
over the sea wall into the sea.

LIZ BLUR

I press my hook
nose into her "boobies."

"You're no wash-up," I say.
Her eyes shift to blur.

I bow, curse,
beg forgiveness.

She snaps
shut my breathing book.

MARCH ANNA MOFFO DREAM

Again I meet Anna Moffo:
she mocks my jackanapes face.

I accompany her in a fake
recital, also real,

and shirk sexual
possibilities to hear

and hear her
hectic hysteric attitude.

As she confidentially
critiques Corelli's crude

instrument, suddenly her gestures
grow expressive, assured,

worth the acclaim
already hers: once more

she rises, tall phoenix,
to record-cover status.

Not once in our conversation
does she invoke my betrayal.

Great ladies never stoop
to notice pusillanimity.

JANE EYRE JICKY

Jane Eyre approaches my Jicky,
sniffs the tiny bottle.

"It's perfume," I warn, "not cognac."
Ignoring me, she drinks.

"Tastes good," she decides,
then calls me "witch"—

inbred interloper. Breaches
and improprieties pile up.

POND JICKY

I pour my Jicky in a dingy pond—
expensive, to waste perfume,

though it is special "pond Jicky,"
with refill opportunities.

Waiting to begin
my long-deferred speech

in the drafty mess hall, one century ago,
I say "ecstasy" and nearly mean it.

PLATO SAYS

Plato says I should write about Plato.
Later I call back, wanting details.

Blank, blank. Julie Andrews enters my apartment,
singing a TV special. She wears a red bathrobe.

Up close, through the camera, I see
Julie's pretty face, see my mother

seeing it, wonder if indeed there are differences
between women, echelons of loveliness.

Julie tells the story of the small rowboat.
Afraid of denouements, I block my ears.

FOUR NEUTRALITIES

FLORIDA SUITE

Before falling asleep I heard on the radio
Delius's *Florida Suite*.

Neutrality
is my new benchmark.

My grandfather moonlighted
as SAT coach.

On his Florida condo wall
he hung John Masefield's autograph, framed.

Observe the permanent stain
on my soul: *neglectful*.

MY BAD VERBS

In the steam room
Craig complimented my butt

and touched it once in the shower.
He said, "I've always wanted to do this."

He managed a restaurant.
He died of double pneumonia.

I must clean up my language.
Listen to my bad verbs!

INVERT DREAM

"Freebies" that weren't free
littered the hotel room.

Slowly I defecated in the tub
while a woman intruder watched,

the moment
neither my best nor my worst.

A short book about Erik Satie
sits on a shelf

the dried-blood color of a stereo
the Emporium sold in the 1960s.

Eagerness lived at that
dark department store.

So did the category "treats"
and the sage calm of a windswept surface.

UNMENTIONABLES

BOOSTER SHOT

The building where Eleanor Roosevelt lived
from 1942 through 1949

is where I got my hepatitis B booster shot.
Where such habits come from I don't know.

In my dream, Steve's father looked like Harry Belafonte.
Wearing running shorts

he approached our restaurant table.
Father and son's faces played

variations on the same skin tone.
Much became transparent

as I watched other patrons ogle Steve's father.
Much became mute and unmentionable.

BABY FOOD

My stairwell smells like Gerber's:
pear, apple, liver, lamb.

Small jars pop when opened—
not a botulism pop, but a pop of perfect peace.

Baby food's vitamins are a green
Schwinn bike stolen because left unlocked.

Each word proves me a brat—
a startled fawn, not philosophical

enough—the most pea-brained man
I've ever met, and the most malleable.

JOLLY FIVE & TEN

Piano teacher stood me up:
holding Schoenberg, I waited in snow.

As consolation, I bought a Corigliano CD.
Fresh-faced composer, Italian son: the concept turns me on.

Five, I played fingerpaints with Marge, my mother's friend.
I bought her *A Guide to Contract Bridge*, for Xmas,

at Jolly Five & Ten. Its book rack twirled.
Or do I wish in retrospect it twirled?

I like making word
cubes, cosy rosaries.

Dream of flight and then rescind ascent:
fool, how dare you soar.

LITTLE FILMS BY FIRELIGHT

RIM JOB

Beacons lit past twilight remind me of slow
snare drums neglecting to commence their rat-a-tat-tat.

Hic et nunc says the frog,
its voice autonomous in morning fog.

WALPURGISNACHT

Canaries wear Hesperidian happy-people costumes,
Mom wears a Marco Polo shirt.

Jesus, in the faint middle, is difficult to see,
touched or defaced by instructional tools.

The Virgin has b.o.
but she explains the world,

a remarkable text with 184 items
and descriptions of where to put them.

Reluctant to step forward until the kingdom falls,
your professor of fable and straw

senses heaviness in the table—
weight that could easily reverse:

landedness could become aerial,
palace could advance to hovel.

I was traveling to Troy. Translate this
into Persian or Basque, it might sound identical.

THANK YOU

Stable truth thanks you for thinking of it.
Stabs in the dark don't go far toward wonder.

Violins stare at me clunking down stairs.
Thoreau wore stripes without thinking "stripe."

II

SUPER 8

Liszt blended ersatz Hungarian experience
  and French hotel sensibility
(stale seminal linen)
  to fashion transcendental études I may
one day play if I can figure out
  how to relax my wrist
and make the page an unbordered
  Super 8 adventure starring Parker Tyler as fisherman
of souls and Greta Garbo as Simone Weil
  staying alone at Hotel Sacher
where cathexis and analysis
  interminable were invented
and my favorite sleeping pill
  Trazodone
which an American baroque poet agrees
  impedes cognition
and gives an Emersonian transparent-eyeball
  morning-after headache
this description courtesy of a prof named Porte
  who lectured me on manure
in the work of Henry David Thoreau

what a detour this poem has become!
not the usual odyssey
    through the modern unconscious
with music by Elmer Bernstein
    a Ross Hunter production starring Susan Kohner
reprising her *Imitation of Life* role
    as "passing" showgirl daughter
I dreamt of a fifties chanteuse
    à la Peggy Lee or Julie London
her name was Clea Vage
    Clea owned a beach house
in Queens and published a book of poems
    called *Liner Notes*
why is someone outside mowing his lawn
    at twelve midnight in December
why isn't that fool in bed
    reading new interpretations
of the Bay of Pigs?
    I feel guilty fleeing the city
to spend the night in the country
    far from terrorism fears
to write a poem I linger outside time
    perhaps in an elevator
a mambo club

East 51st or Gotham Book Mart
a back room
  Tower Records Bed Bath and Beyond
the subway, Q or N or L
  the lines I never take
because I don't know where they go
  or why and when they stop
in my dream the M5 bus
  took me from Rockaway to a beach house
not Clea Vage's but Marianne Moore's
  and her tetchy Mom's
they discussed rhinos and pedophiles
  at their last seance
which I attended dressed as Valentino
  my *Son of the Sheik*
costume bought at a Santa Monica yard sale in 1955
  before I was born
Steve's potential client the French wine importer
  first name pronounced "Yvonne"
wants to build an escapist modernismo
  maisonette on 23 acres
Steve likes butter more than I do
  I prefer confiture
served in polished silver bowls with espresso spoons

we ate perfect jam
near a Dordogne water mill
an ill lady slept on a sofa
while we consumed confiture
this hotel famous for fruit jam
though a reputation founded on jam
is perforce a limited renown
at night I can speak freely
authority no longer a distant colonized isle
toward which I veer with broken sail
days I sleepwalk
like Liz in *Boom!* demanding
"Injection!" or the tranquilizer
shot in *Suddenly, Last Summer*
after she accidentally wanders
into the lobotomy rec room
where the mad-beyond-repair
rock and suckle stuffed animals
forgive these fetishes
in my childhood's living room
hung a reproduction Soyer painting
three female dancers
I mistook for three lunatics
on coffee break

lounging in a mental asylum corridor
I feared their splayed skinny torpid limbs
     when my father
first used the word "schizophrenia"
     in my presence he defined it
as a grown woman afraid to get
     off the toilet
because outside her bathroom
     enemies lie in wait
as a youth I made two dramatic movies
     with my Super 8 camera
The American Time Bomb
     premiered at our avant-garde seder
and *What Men Live By*
     based on a Tolstoy fairy tale
my other films were realistic reportage
     older brother on a horsie
close-up of my baby brother crying
     as he flees two taunting kids
why didn't I protect him?
     close-up of my baby sister crying
topless in our backyard's plastic wading pool
     the provocation unclear

ELEGY FOR EVERYONE

Henry James mysteriously ball-wounded
in dream tries *Dove sono*
as spoken-word performance poem.

Air France thinks me Italian terrorist.
Playing virginal in Paris
I attempt complete sentences.

Buy white futurist sunglasses?
Join psychoanalytic institute in spare time?
May art continue month to month

episodic like *Perils of Pauline?*
"The history of the world is the history of pain"
I said after root canal, Place Vendôme.

Baby licks shovel, drops it on ground.
Mother picks it up for baby's sake.
Baby drops it again. Mother picks it up.

Repetez, s'il vous plaît.
I need a set of measuring spoons:
measurement's my mantra.

Isn't God in Old English
he who measures?
Would I be a good adoptive father?

Walter Benjamin's clots
mix commentary and quotation.
Does *konvolut* mean faggot,

cluster, or complication?
Lita, actress opposite me in *Tinder Box*:
in her presence for the first time

I used the word *orgy*
and waited to be rescued
by a camp counseler who would understand my underage

melancholy profundity in Los Gatos—
osteoporosis-stooped mountains.
Handsome men have an obligation to be humble

to offset their beauty's aggressiveness.
Why for hours has a woman
sat on a step block-lettered DO NOT SIT?

Brother's upstairs room became mother's room
and minimally father's. I read
Rosemary's Baby on staircase to "the upstairs"

while mother, in hospital, had abortion.
Pierre Bourdieu died, my grandmother died.
June Jordan died, R. W. B. Lewis died.

In 19th century my broken tooth
wouldn't lead to death:
I'd be just another Paris

wanderer with bandaged head.
I dislike the word *partner*
though the person who occupies

that position is divine . . .
Exactly midlife, I've failed
to describe simultaneity.

OBSERVATIONS

Yesterday's newspaper said
in a writer's life
there is no such thing as "wasted time."

Dream: my shrink relaxed her former
med-school rigidity, near the Fens.
At least I've broken

rhetoric's back,
after five years' treadmill.
My sister's cinephilia:

she wanted to see *Yours, Mine, and Ours*
(starring Lucille Ball)
more than a parched land wants rain.

Dream: my mother had a baby.
I wasn't the baby.
It was a different creature, smaller.

I watched my mother protect
and ignore it
not because my mother was evil

but because she was fatigued.
You can tell when cauliflower is cooked:
it starts to smell like cauliflower.

Rule of thumb:
vegetables are done
when they smell like themselves.

The rule applies to kale, spinach, broccoli,
potatoes. Onions, however,
smell like onions long before they are finished.

I dreamt Elizabeth Hardwick
corrected my verbs—
she told me, "Instead of *is*, we use *lead* or *invite*."

Twenty-four years ago
driving into New York I said
"This city's electric!":

I was thinking of Anaïs Nin,
her diaries
my paragon of literary ecstasy.

Maybe I'm a horrible
teacher: in class
I mentioned "syncopation."

Why does my shrink insist
on communication?
Admire Alair Gomes for photographing

hairy thighs in Rio ten thousand times
and not selling the images—
donating them to a library.

Dream: en route
to interviewing Liz Taylor
I met her handsome son,

outline of buttocks visible through blue jeans.
(Later he turned out to be an impostor.)
I kept Liz waiting fifteen minutes

while I dilly-dallied with her "son."
If I resemble my mother
that's not catastrophic.

Some poets don't have a past,
only a present (silver light on leaf).
It's possible to see me

through an unflattering telescope
and hate the vista,
consider it *the already seen.*

III

JOHN WAYNE'S PERFUMES

In *Cast a Giant Shadow*, John Wayne wore Claiborne Sport;
  in *Flame of the Barbary Coast*, Femme;
    Dakota, Diorissimo.

In *The Undefeated*, John Wayne wore Unzipped;
  in *Overland Stage Raiders*, Opium;
    Stagecoach, Snuff.

In *The Alamo*, John Wayne wore Anaïs Anaïs;
  in *Jet Pilot*, Joop Nuit d'Été;
    Chisum, Charlie.

In *Barbarian and the Geisha*, John Wayne wore Baby Doll;
  in *Wake of the Red Witch*, White Diamonds;
    Baby Face, Boss.

In *How the West Was Won*, John Wayne wore Hugo Deep Red;
  in *His Private Secretary*, Halston Sheer;
    Rio Lobo, Realities.

In *Lady Takes a Chance*, John Wayne wore Lucky You;
  in *Sands of Iwo Jima*, Sun Moon and Stars;
    Hatari, Happy.

ARCADES FASHION PROJECT #1:
THE CASSANDRA CROSSING *(1976)*

Ava Gardner wore her yellow seersucker exposé,
Richard Harris wore his bamboo dialectic sandals,
Sophia Loren wore her iron demolition slacks,
and I wore my brown net boredom.

Burt Lancaster wore his orange conspiracy boots,
Martin Sheen wore his black Baudelaire,
Ingrid Thulin wore her shiny anthropological nihilism,
and I dreamt of the striped future.

Lee Strasberg wore her idle leather,
O. J. Simpson wore his zippered velvet prostitution,
Alida Valli wore her Marx green shantung photography jeans
and her fake spotted leopard automaton,

Carlo Ponti wore his pink social movement ascot,
and I wore my opalescent red Jung theory of progress.

BEST-SELLING JEWISH PORN FILMS

Jewish Gold
Jews Between Themselves
Wet Jew Stories
Jewish Jocks

Casa Jew
Jew-in-the-Hood
jewboyz.com
Sweatin' Jew

Jewish Hard Drive
Da Bronx Jew
Jewish Sex Party
Domination Jewish Wrestling

Jewish Locker-Room Rumble
King-Size Jew
Jewish Hotel Hell
Jewish Heat Waves

Jews Should Do It!
Jews of Company F
All-American Jew
Jewish Trucking Co.

Jewish Tool & Die
Hot Jewish Rods
Jewish House Memories
Fraternity Jews

Jewish Sex Scandal
Jewish Fraternity Gang Bang
Big Jewish Daddy
Everybody Wants My Jewish Dick

Jewish Monuments
Jewish Sex Machine
Stiff Jewish Stuff
Jewish Buddies

Jews Next Door
Barebacking Jews
Genuine Leather Jews
Working Stiff Jews

Jewish Uprising
Jewish Twinks
Legendary Jewish Bodies
College Jewish Swim Team

Jewish Body Storm
Jewish Wrestle Club
Tight Jewish Assets
Jews in the Sand

Diary of a Jewish Sex Fiend
Solo Jewish Sex—Extended Pleasure for Men
The Ultimate Jewish Male Climax!
Total Jewish Corruption

Fallen Jewish Angel
The Isle of Jewish Men
Jewish Oral Exams
The Jewish Pizza Boy: He Delivers

Three Jewish Brothers
Jewish Room Service
Jewish Sexual Healing
Jews Beg for Mercy

DING AN SICH

Penis my mother
once gave me for my birthday.

Rib cage of close
reading "The Idiot Boy."

Esophagus of assigning
my students a short essay on walking.

Kneecap of sudden nose-
dive into anti-sublimity.

Fibula of not
fearing cancer.

Breastbone of watching
Berlin Alexanderplatz (lousy print).

Ulnar nerve of Elmer's glue
and Brad my large-skulled misfit mate in 1969.

Penis of rebirth
and don't let it happen again.

IN THIS VALE OF TEARS WE CALL EXISTENCE

in this bizarre carnival I call my human life
in this domestic habitation I call the fourth Spice Girl
in this failure I call yesterday
in this manhood I call Bakelite bracelet or a dame I knew wearing one
in this glade I call my firm young globes

in this green scrimshaw I call japanned countertop
in this breakfast room I call an opportunity to be a horny third-grader
in this Antabuse I call Catholicism
in this mother-in-law I call marriage
in this freedom from supervision I call February

in this Rhonda I call lover
in this girl's pink pullover turtleneck I call mainstreaming
in this sloe-eyed bystander I call Romanticism's long-overdue revolt
    against modernity
in this editor I call fatso
in this fatso I call protector of the sacredness (once) of french fries

in this radioactivity I call brother
in this adequacy I call dick

in this Queen Mother I call deadbeat
in this cognac I call *Carnaval*
in this wilderness I call early death from TB

in this genital mutilation I call rickrack
in this gender I call "No Pets"
in this Manolo Blahnik high heel I call rear-entry intercourse
in this intercrural congress I call fastidiousness
in this retro mentality I call *assiette variée*

in this idiom I call *interruptus*
in this Robert Altman I call Victory Garden
in this Vienna I call Orangina
in this Exxon Valdez oil spill I call sugar high
in this U.S. Post Office employee I call ball-and-chain

in this Lalique vase I call adiposity
in this opened iris I call foul-smelling discharge
in this wino I call *Mimesis*
in this purple flannel bathrobe I call trusting your boyfriend to call
    the shots
in this inhibition I call string of Xmas lights

in this catarrh I call democracy
in this excuse me I call rape perhaps
in this string of pearls I call your 1960s
in this Bermuda paradise I call public urination
in this grab bag I call my uterus (hello?)

in this pot belly I call lecture
in this straight football player I call micropenis
in this Ben Affleck I call my shaved neck
in this bar of soap I call cigarette
in this oops! I call love

in this crocodile briefcase I call nuclear preparedness
in this fleeting eye contact I call chiasmus
in this multiplication table I call "no no no no no!"
in this educational filmstrip I call cleft palate
in this M4M cruising website I call parturition

in this Shorty I call Julia Child
in this cute seminarian I call blow job
in this lamplit hair salon I call brutality in South Boston
in this Catwoman I call interpretation
in this Washington D.C. I call laugh and clap your hands

in this sorta nice interview I call smell of pork loin
in this beauty mark I call reform Jew
in this nickel-and-dime-ing I call drive through Bois de Boulogne
in this manicurist's newsletter I call grip of the past
in this torrent I call sausage

in this retard I call faggot
in this Giuliani I call La Guardia
in this wash-and-set I call church
in this vernacular I call not particularly quotable
in this choking victim I call book

in this garnet ring I call glottal stop
in this egg I call vibrator
in this anxiety I call taxi
in this dust bunny I call some people
in this beige pantsuit I call inept direction

in this Yvette Mimieux I call coq au vin
in this I I call you
in this aptness I call Stanley Kaplan
in this doo-wop I call maya
in this oldster I call wisdom literature

in this gamelan I call ideas

in this buzz cut I call trumpet lick

in this ether I call ear

in this smart aleck I call I must prepare a list for you

in this artifice I call law

IV

CREVICES

I can't tell apart
human beings and lawn ornaments.
More, later, about my vast holdings.

★

Oh, if I kept notebooks
proving New York sidewalks
were not imaginary!

★

Footnote:
rain floods my boat.
I lack overcoat.

★

I am a tiny topic,
though misanthropic,
like snowy peripeteia on a butte.

★

I wonder what my mother felt
when the doctor told her the baby was dead.
Not my business—but I think about it some mornings.

Two phrases I'm dying
to say are "hack pianism"
and "son at a glance."

★

My humor
is running out
or is "rum."

★

Why don't I mention
box hedges again,
or buxom, or pudendum?

★

I dislike "hot"
(stolen) cognizance,
including my own.

★

Current events:
my sadomasochistic student
has the smarts for me. (Better than the hots.)

★

I fainted on Monte Antico—
no, I drank it.
I sing fever on the river Po.

★

Later, I might sing sinus
congestion, the word "unpanoplied,"
and these harlequin shackles.

BALLAD OF THE LAYETTE

Sing a song of Baby's illiteracy.
Words hit consciousness
and vanquish formulae.

★

Sing a song of Baby's European layette.
Nanny collapsed,
awed, in a heap on the floor.

★

Sing a song of deadbeat dads,
impoverished barnyard creatures,
logic only I can follow.

★

Sing a song of Baby's future—
talent scouts and holding pens,
Rachmaninoff and road rage.

★

Baby lacks the proper
aural sifting mechanism.
His mind lays out for me alone its platter of goodies.

DECEPTIONS OF MIDNIGHT

I don't want my students
to get the wrong idea
when they see my blue
nipples pointing to the moon.

★

I love art
history: if only
I were
not exploding!

★

A short
aubade:
"The world is tired,
lacquered."

★

I cut the words
"and yet"
and meditate
on the excision—

it takes hours
to perform
the surgery,
hours to recover.

★

Was anyone kind
to my mother
when I was an infant?
Could I have been kinder?

Don't consider me a martyr
worth going to heaven
just because now I say
I aimed to be kind.

STORIES OF O

Don't bother
being charming!

X-rays of my skull
reveal an early

marriage
to a dwarf.

Devotedly yours,
The Author.

★

I rode a goddess
six flights to heaven.

She guessed my trade—
alphabet acolyte—

and lit my bluebeard
window. O

holy lay.
Perfume by Patou.

I drank her grudge.
She crossed my Rialto,

★

inserted a rectal
thermometer: not the end

of the world. Objects
need breaking in.

It sounds euphoric.
O turn away

but also be
my golem.

THE VISIBLE

"From a distance
it is perfectly visible,"

she said of her vagina.
"God put it rather high."

It's not her fault
she has no taste.

★

Drugged, she took a bus
to visit me: how loyal.

She cooked me an omelette,
derided my usual meals:

"Your idea of dinner
is cold cuts!"

★

Her son died.
Her son was sexy.

Her son had a wife.
Her son had a built-in pool.

I sat by the son's poolside.
I touched the son in the dark.

From a distance
he was perfectly visible.

SPA MOODS

A spa mood hits. I duck.
It goes away.

I sit up.
It hits again.

Why not swing
wide the door?

★

A pinhead
whose ontology

needs burping,
I lean on

this instant's
impromptu

scaffolding—
and it falls.

★

I wish I could claim
victory, but I hate

to organize
steam clouds.

★

Eclectic pastoral:
I'm wearing

too much makeup,
or not enough.

I miss confetti,
lacunae. Pals,

I'm on a premonition
streak: please slap me.

HOW TO BEND

Patio furniture, plastic
and filthy, assists

pedagogy's colonoscopy
always in the airport,

according to the sluggish melodrama
Triumvirate Purloins Lemonade.

★

Elevator shaft's black rain
bends the cover

of the how-to manual.
How to what?

★

"I'm a kid, too," I want
to shout, in complicitous foreboding,

backstage on a small lunar shallop.
And we will consider it a pleasant experience.

MOVIES ENDING BY THE SEA

No one understands:
I want negation.

And what of my mother?
Didn't she discover me?

Didn't she fold
bath towels and washcloths?

Is it too late to enroll
in a Great Books college

so I can torture myself
with erudition?

Many movies end
with seaside scenes:

★

I starred in a maritime documentary
depicting small boats versus large,

sailors within sailors—
a must-see,

though not about prose or poetry,
mostly about truncation,

a variety of valor,
like not getting out of bed.

★

Someone in the screening
room "stook up"

for my mother, said
not nice things about her son:

Where is his appetite?
Please pour a petite

★

geyser of flattery
on my forehead.

I lack
emotional thoroughness—

hence the sea's
sidereal farewell.

THE MICKEY MOUSE FOREPLAY REEL

I want a firmer way
to begin this sentence—
instead of "I"
a dateless residence:

★

I showed the crowd
an impressive film—
the Mickey Mouse foreplay reel.
Nothing mattered

★

except nightfall's promptness,
escritoire with many minute drawers
in a shop window,
a price fathomless

★

yet I almost reached the intersection, where the neighborhood

became intolerant,

momently exhibiting

a relationship to porridge, to borderline catatonic . . .

CURRENT EVENTS

Last night I dreamt of Burkina Faso.

★

Sometimes I call my mother "Bob."

★

The first poem I ever wrote concerned a bicycle.

★

My New York neighborhood is sunny San Diego.

★

My friend was murdered last week in South Africa
while visiting an escort
parlor. He didn't seek early death.
He merely asked for steam.
Did I already say? His name was Greg
and the guy who told me about the massacre is Josh.

FEMALE MASCULINITY

Two guys sucking each other in the steam room
didn't want anything
to do with me, evidently—
I left them to their comedy.

★

Legato longings:
wish for walnuts, wish for water,
wish to exorcise this morning's debauch—
two Fauré nocturnes.

★

In slow motion
Steve tussled with a motorcycle
trying to run me over
on the boulevard of moon smut

splicing together bridges
and lagoons, like the bride

of Frankenstein rushing
to overtake the inert

Real, a mass
of facts, some conjugal,
some comic—
contrapuntal tenebrae!

TWO REARS

PORTRAY GSTAAD AS ENTELECHY'S OPPOSITE

Your anus, only
in the dream, had pharmacological
undyingness, like Ray Stark
feeling his way toward a remake.

I envy
what the mother's elemental
tar reflects
of a sky not crosshatched with replacement's wings.

GLEANINGS FROM GERSHOM SCHOLEM

His butt, mine, differences
rarely sung:

imagine receiving
a moral spanking,

a gravechant's
gage thrown down.

His night's
microscopic script unleavens the last extant code.

TWO LITTLE ELEGIES FOR JOE BRAINARD

I.

I sit awake all night
watching a ladybug
cross the windowpane.

The tower of Babel
at my fingertips
bewitches her.

I've wasted my forties—
today's the second
morning of my fortieth year.

Oh, but I must mention
one rare red record,
found at a flea market:

"The Rosary," sung
by Vivian Della Chiesa.
It holds up.

2.

At the great soprano's husband's funeral
the synagogue smells of talc and hair oil.

I wear a tie with chromosomal squiggles
and read "Kubla Khan" while waiting for the service

to begin. My grail is intersection,
though I can't hold it,

don't know what it is—
mysterious sadness falling into neat piles.

V

PIERROT LUNAIRE

I. MOONDRUNK

"my skin, except in dreams, is antiseptic"
a student sends me his novel, idiomatic, adorable, but needing vast
  correction
Bette Davis wears a guilt-inducing outfit
most of her face covered by a fur hat

Mae West stands to receive applause, primarily boos
crying, she goes mad, slashes right and left, then ceremoniously dies
"my skin, except in dreams, is antiseptic"
a student sends me his novel, idiomatic, adorable, but needing vast
  correction

Eve Arden, seated in my row, archly nods and genuflects
alluding to her Miss Brooks role
which I pretend to remember so she won't be offended
I say hi to a freak with scab-caked fingers after ignoring his crib all
  night
"my skin, except in dreams, is antiseptic"

my shrink brings sweetbreads dressed in raspberry vinegar to the
    backyard potluck
also mâche, which she tosses with her hands
the sweetbreads taste fat-free, a saltless panache
not a desirable dish but magically nutritious

sweetbreads advertise her quixotic prudence
and surpass the crappy barbecue served in my quadrant
my shrink brings sweetbreads dressed in raspberry vinegar to the
    backyard potluck
also mâche, which she tosses with her hands

my brother scissors off a tulip's head
a chemical condition fools him into thinking his deed salutary surgery
he gratuitously slays healthy flowers
under the guise of bringing them to life
my shrink brings sweetbreads dressed in raspberry vinegar to the
    backyard potluck

Patty Duke is (apparently) black
we wear the same red Prada shoes but mine are scuffed and faded
a person who looks like Patty Duke serves as my babysitter
this fact comes up in conversation with Patty Duke

I make a snide remark about Patty Duke in front of Patty Duke
not entirely knowing that Patty Duke is present
Patty Duke is (apparently) black
we wear the same red Prada shoes but mine are scuffed and faded

problem: I don't telegraph my pathos or frame it analytically
Patty Duke frowns when I praise her aphorisms
she suffers a memory lapse and takes a repeat to mask her error
for whose benefit the charade?
Patty Duke is (apparently) black

my mother in her sixties gives birth to twins
definitive proof of miraculousness
Diana Vreeland drops by for dinner
uninvited, she brings one cucumber and one tomato

hastily I add scallions and curry to the soup pot
within the dream I tell this dream to a feminist linguist
my mother in her sixties gives birth to twins
definitive proof of miraculousness

in *Vogue* Diana Vreeland reads about the meal or the trend it represents
the very meal I'm serving her, which makes me persona non grata
yet also an avatar of revolutionary panic
Diana Vreeland grants me access to her parka as if we're still in
    Vietnam
my mother in her sixties gives birth to twins

the Madonna resembles a raptor, but *relatedness* (Winnicott, Klein?)
   shines in her eyes
object relations intact for the kiddies
she sews a quilt celebrating gay marriage
and wears a paper dress below a cardboard wig

out comes a shiny deck of Holocaust playing cards
on their backs I scribble private correspondences and fairy-tale longings
the Madonna resembles a raptor, but *relatedness* (Winnicott, Klein?)
   shines in her eyes
object relations intact for the kiddies

I glimpse her son's morphed penis, hugely controversial
atmospheric sepia haze conceals our genital kinship
our sonic manners faulty, Schoenberg seguing into Aphex Twin
her cut-out dress the most womanly object in the composition
the Madonna resembles a raptor, but *relatedness* (Winnicott, Klein?)
   shines in her eyes

6. CROSSES

sitting beside Susan Sontag at a dinner party, an elliptical table
I hold a copy of *Death Kit*, which sends me back in time to an earlier
    dream
visit to her apartment, a long intimate chat about memoir
I mention a minor character who resembles the author

this reference revives her attentiveness
I ask her to autograph *Death Kit* though observers think I'm
    brown-nosing
sitting beside Susan Sontag at a dinner party, an elliptical table
I hold a copy of *Death Kit*, which sends me back in time to an earlier
    dream

I ask if her novel is veiled autobiography
afraid this interpretation won't please her
so far I see on her face no signs irreversibly saturnine
in the dream I tell her I'm writing poems tangentially touched by
    Pierrot
sitting beside Susan Sontag at a dinner party, an elliptical table

liquid trickles down Virginia Woolf's leg in the fancy detox clinic lobby
only my boyfriend understands the trickle's secret meaning
on an emergency telephone we call the maid, who brings a tray of
    snifters
unfortunately there's not enough cognac to go around

in Woolf's vicinity a Liberace lookalike flashes a self-published book
    of poems
he hides his Yiddishkeit in a plastic shopping bag and spouts
    fraudulent koans
liquid trickles down Virginia Woolf's leg in the fancy detox clinic lobby
only my boyfriend understands the trickle's secret meaning

the nurse says my bank account contains ninety dollars, not nine
    hundred
the zero omitted, she claims, "for my own good"
why is my mother eating a chicken-versus-egg sandwich in the parked
    Jaguar
and why does the Liberace lookalike rhyme "green" with "kerosene"?
liquid trickles down Virginia Woolf's leg in the fancy detox clinic lobby

8. SERENADE

I give birth but the baby survives a mere few hours
film footage of my ordeal premieres behind the makeshift altar
I'm positive that Desi Arnaz Jr. is the solution
minus the hypotenuse of Desi Senior's regard

on a Roman street a gypsy child hawks lemon soap
she won't let me smell it first so I refuse to buy
I give birth but the baby survives a mere few hours
film footage of my ordeal premieres behind the makeshift altar

the soap looks decent but it might be disguised meatballs
from the Carnegie Hall bathroom I overhear the debutante clang her
    appassionata
a rickety children's choir advocates appeasement
on the recurring afternoon of JFK's assassination
I give birth but the baby survives a mere few hours

a dying drunk expatriate I'd shunned now hugs a theory festschrift
honoring Said or Schoenberg and containing Colorforms or
    chloroform
euphemistic, she says "my little sickness"
curled on her bedroom kilim, she clutches the book to please her dead
    mother

my visit censures the expat's terminal trance
her face unruined despite drink's inroads
a dying drunk expatriate I'd shunned now hugs a theory festschrift
honoring Said or Schoenberg and containing Colorforms or
    chloroform

I listen to an Anna Moffo record of a Tennessee Williams opera
a long recitative death, like Butterfly but better
I crave lemon curd tart but communicate a wish for poppy seed
and must accept the humdrum substitute
a dying drunk expatriate I'd shunned now hugs a theory festschrift

after my tonsils come out my mother wears a wedding dress with red
    appliqué
I pretend to discover a new way to do the Twist
and write a tiny gibberish poem about how to straddle the line between
    soul and toy
schmaltz splashes on my leg and I watch a film called *Bette and Boy*

Prada opens a baby boutique selling booties and "onesies"
the salesman says "your cologne has a bad aftersmell"
after my tonsils come out my mother wears a wedding dress with red
    appliqué
I pretend to discover a new way to do the Twist

a suburban vintner runs a regressive sex ring
his adult tricks not allowed to speak until he diapers them
an all-seeing editor sets fire to my first draft
she doesn't want its unfinished face to haunt me in the future
after my tonsils come out my mother wears a wedding dress with red
    appliqué

VI

TO A MAPLE

Green leaves outside my window
your shaped droplets
are nothing I can describe.

Birds eye you
moving up and down, a weighty pubis.
You have a conscience.

I pity you,
lenient exhibitionists
dependent on a flake.

Amid crossbreeze
fruitlessly I regret
my snobbish indiscretions.

Leaves, continue to be
anti-Vichy, and to weather
my inanimate temperament.

O HOMES ACROSS THE BAY

O homes across the bay,
quiet, manly homes,

bear with me: I see
daffodils on your front lawns,

grape hyacinths, too,
forsythia, delirium tremens,

banquets at stingy taverns and then returns
with Mother to the neat and single room,

attentions given to potential girlfriend,
her praise tattooed on my left arm!

BRAHMS PIANO QUARTET NO. 1

Brahms dreamt
the complacent
girl's allergy to calamine
lotion screwed up her cat's
psyche. Clara's
hubby had a writing
block, which threatened
the Chinese dinner *en famille.*
Insensate, whorish,
the taxi failed to bring me here.
The hoodlum gang
coalesced. The dime
novel mugged
the Madonna of the Postpartum
Exasperation, a rain of
alphabet-soup letters alighting
on a background landscape's pinched fronds.

DREGS OF THE MIOCENE EPOCH

She witnessed five minutes of patriarchy
but then the five minutes were over
and she lost interest.
She took her jack-o'-lantern and exited.
I'd failed.

At the next bacchanal
she gave me incomplete
laxation.

The result?
I discovered (again) a nemesis—
household arts open to the water hemlocks.

I ended up a barterer, a nondescript
nightstick.
What a pity.

DIVA ATONEMENT TOUR

I hate the psyche.
Cloudy today: brown, carmine, not blue.

I'm having a devilish time
controlling my body's

two gods:
theatric, tutelary.

Last night I decided again
to be a maniac, risking brain

fever, like my father,
whose temperature once rose to 108:

impressive. In our house,
only the sick were great.

SMELLY COOKIES

A mother, Bertie,
baked smelly
butter cookies:

confusing
conflations of snack
and stink bomb,

they saved me
from glossolalia's
wet evening glove.

Comic strips isolate
their merely
theoretical heroines,

as you, cookies,
are estranged from today
and its heavy, doubled lilacs.

WATER MUSIC

Let's regain the simplicity
of Jello 1-2-3,
lonely Polish airs, Dear
John letters to nerve-damaged cadets.

I smell my grandfather
Joe's pipe tobacco in the elevator
as I ride down to the damp basement
(he's been dead twelve years).

Summer. Time to drown
my senses in the souk's convolvulus.
Observe my skittering foolishness, like fish
in shallow bioluminescent bays.

The last movement suspends
development in favor of "dinky"
recapitulation, though tonic
and subdominant are more than bric-a-brac.

Tomorrow I'll see my father again—
he'll dismiss me. I'll dismiss him, too:
counterpoint, first theme, second theme.
No one asks why I lie

down like a high-school sophomore in the goat
position. Staggering, my ignorance
of contemporary lust formations,
a dirge composed of oars, claims, trees, tame owls.

GERMAN ROMANTIC SONG

Cryptic owl on my sill,
olive branch in the gold-bowered cope,

when I was a child I didn't know
what the word "colleague" meant: darkness?
My father had many colleagues;
I had none.

I told his assistant, twenty-one years ago,
"I wonder which I love most,
words or music."
I can't remember her advice,
though later she sued my father—
a long story. Perhaps
ecstasy can't be sought?
Materialism is no longer my amour,
I'm forever a bridegroom to bliss and its disguises.

ACKNOWLEDGMENTS

The author thanks the editors of the following publications, in which these po-
ems, sometimes in different versions, previously appeared:

110 Stories: New York Writes after September 11, ed. Ulrich Baer (NYU Press,
2002): "Super 8"; *Barrow Street*: *"Ding an sich"*; *Columbia*: "Movies Ending
by the Sea"; *Electronic Poetry Review*: "Ballad of the Layette," "Brahms Pi-
ano Quartet No. 1," "How to Bend," "John Wayne's Perfumes"; *Five Fingers
Review*: "Four Neutralities," "In This Vale of Tears We Call Existence,"
"Observations"; *Fort Necessity*: "Deceptions of Midnight," "Water Music";
Global City Review: "Spa Moods," "The Visible"; *Gulf Coast*: "Bulletins";
Hayden's Ferry Review: "The Collected Works of Slimboy" (from "Breaches
and Improprieties"), "Crevices"; *LIT*: "The Mickey Mouse Foreplay Reel,"
"O Homes Across the Bay"; *LUNGFULL!*: "Female Masculinity"; *Lyric*:
"Dregs of the Miocene Epoch," "Fever on the River Po," "To a Maple"; *Mis-
sissippi Review*: "Arcades Fashion Project #1: *The Cassandra Crossing* (1976),"
"The Pourquoi Club"; *Painted Bride Quarterly*: "Best-Selling Jewish Porn
Films"; *Pequod*: "Unmentionables"; *Ploughshares*: "Diva Atonement Tour,"
"German Romantic Song"; *Pressed Wafer*: "Two Little Elegies for Joe Brain-
ard"; *Triquarterly*: "Stanzas in My 39th Year"; *Verse*: "Current Events," "El-
egy for Everyone"; *Western Humanities Review*: "Pierrot Lunaire."